Alfred's
Easy piano songs
CHRISTMAS

50 HOLIDAY FAVORITES

Produced by
Alfred Music
P.O. Box 10003
Van Nuys, CA 91410-0003
alfred.com

Printed in USA.

ISBN-10: 1-4706-3615-8
ISBN-13: 978-1-4706-3615-9

Cover Photos
Black piano © iStock.com/The AYS

 Alfred Cares. Contents printed on environmentally responsible paper.

contents

TITLE	PAGE

AWAY IN A MANGER

Music by
JAMES R. MURRAY

*Optional: Use dotted bracket measures for intro.

ANGELS WE HAVE HEARD ON HIGH

Joyfully (♩ = 112)

Traditional Carol

BELIEVE

(from *The Polar Express*)

Words and Music by
ALAN SILVESTRI and GLEN BALLARD

Believe - 3 - 1

BLUE CHRISTMAS

Words and Music by
BILL HAYES and JAY JOHNSON

BRING A TORCH, JEANNETTE, ISABELLA

Traditional French Carol

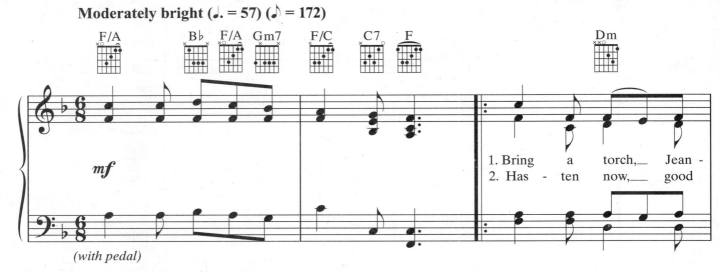

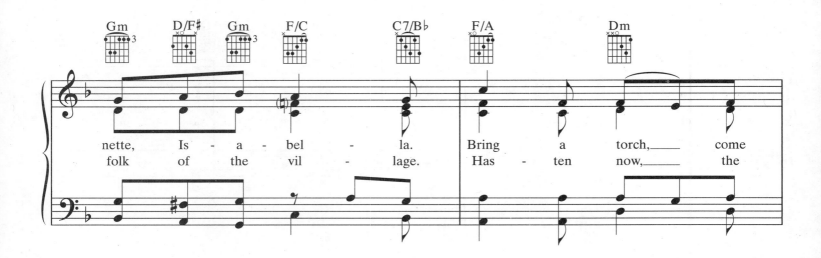

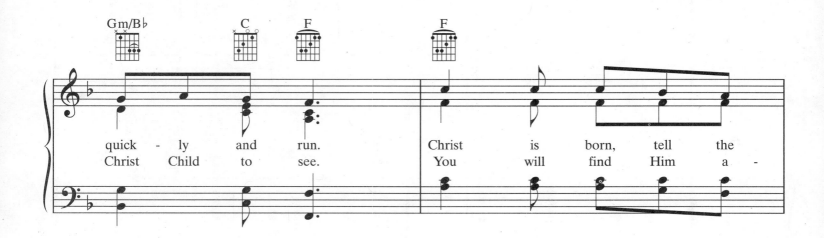

CELEBRATE ME HOME

Lyrics by
KENNY LOGGINS

Music by
KENNY LOGGINS and BOB JAMES

Moderately (♩ = 96) (♫ = ♪³♪)

Verse 1:

1. Home for the hol-i-days, I be-lieve I've missed each and ev-'ry face. Come on and play one eas-y. Let's turn on ev-'ry love light in the place.

It's time I found my-self to-tal-ly sur-round-ed in your cir-cles. Oh, my friends.

A CHILD THIS DAY IS BORN

Words and Music by
WILLIAM SANDYS

Moderately bright (♩ = 120)

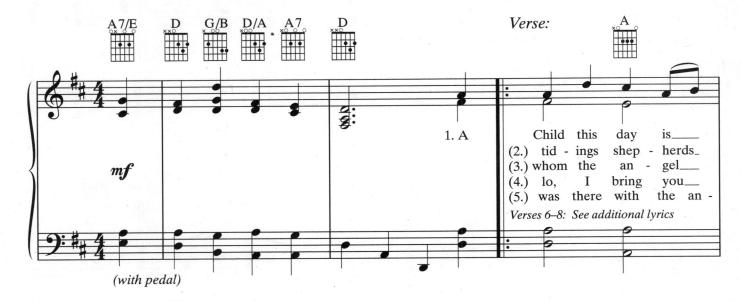

Verse:

1. A Child this day is___
(2.) tid - ings shep - herds___
(3.) whom the an - gel___
(4.) lo, I bring you___
(5.) was there with the an -

Verses 6–8: See additional lyrics

(with pedal)

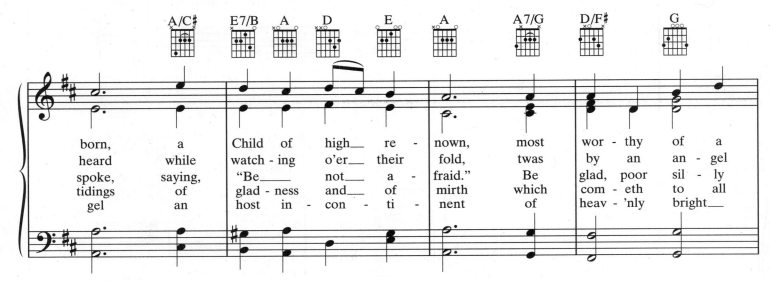

born, a Child of high___ re - nown, most wor - thy of a
heard a while watch - ing o'er___ their fold, most twas by an an - gel
spoke, saying, "Be___ not___ a - fraid." Be glad, poor sil - ly
tidings of glad - ness and___ of mirth which com - eth to all
gel an host in - con - ti - nent which of heav - 'nly bright___

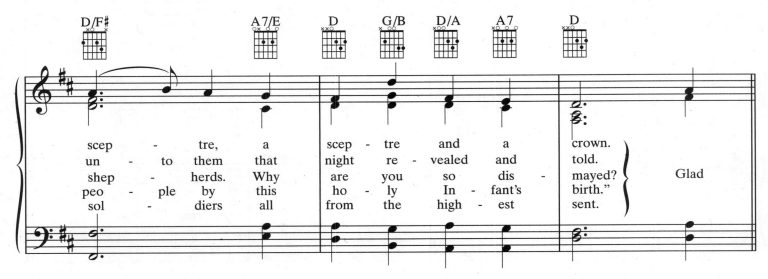

scep - tre, a scep - tre and a crown.
un - to them that night re - vealed and told.
shep - herds. Why are you so dis - mayed? } Glad
peo - ple by this ho - ly In - fant's birth."
sol - diers all from the high - est sent.

A Child This Day Is Born - 2 - 1

Chorus:

tid-ings to all men. Glad tid-ings, sing we

may, be - cause the King of

Kings was born on Christ-mas

Day. born on Christ-mas Day.

2. These
3. To
4. "For
5. Then
6. They
7. And
8. All

rit.

Verse 6:
They praised the Lord, our God
And our celestial King.
All glory be in Paradise,
This heavenly host do sing.
(To Chorus:)

Verse 7:
And as the angel told them,
So to them did appear.
They found the young Child, Jesus Christ
With Mary, his mother dear.
(To Chorus:)

Verse 8:
All glory be to God,
That sitteth still on high
With praises and with triumph great,
And joyful melody.
(To Chorus:)

CHRISTMAS VACATION

(from *National Lampoon's Christmas Vacation*)

Words and Music by
BARRY MANN and CYNTHIA WEIL

Moderately (♩ = 88)

Verse:

1. It's that time,___ Christ - mas - time___ is here.___
2. This old house___ sure is look - in' good.___

Ev - 'ry - bod - y knows___ there's not a bet - ter time___ of year.___
Got our - selves___ the fin - est snow - man in the neigh - bor - hood.___

Hear that sleigh?___ San - ta's on___ his way.___
Ain't it fun,___ al - ways on___ the run?___

Hip, hip, hoo - ray for Christ - mas va - ca - tion.___
That's how it's done on Christ - mas va - ca - tion.___

Christmas Vacation - 3 - 1

Chorus 3:

3. Peace and joy__ and love__ are ev - 'ry - where.

You can feel__ the mag - ic in the air.

Let the spir - it of__ the sea - son car - ry us a - way.__

Hip, hip hoo - ray for Christ - mas va - ca - tion.__

THE COVENTRY CAROL

Moderately slow lullaby (♩ = 108)

Traditional Carol

*Optional: Use dotted bracket measures for intro.

DECK THE HALL

Traditional Welsh Carol

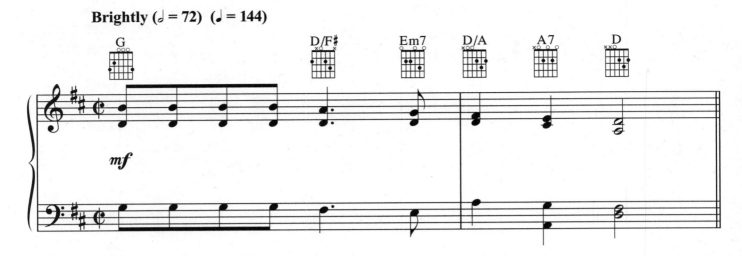

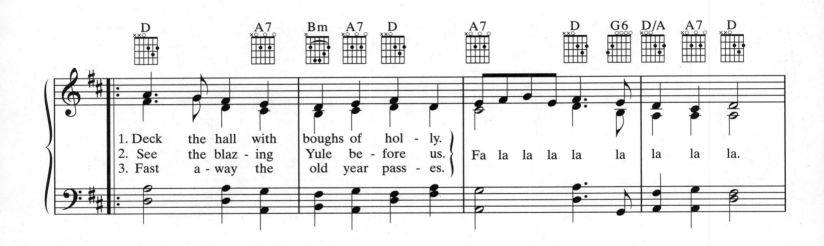

1. Deck the hall with boughs of hol - ly.
2. See the blaz - ing Yule be - fore us.
3. Fast a - way the old year pass - es.
Fa la la la la la la la la.

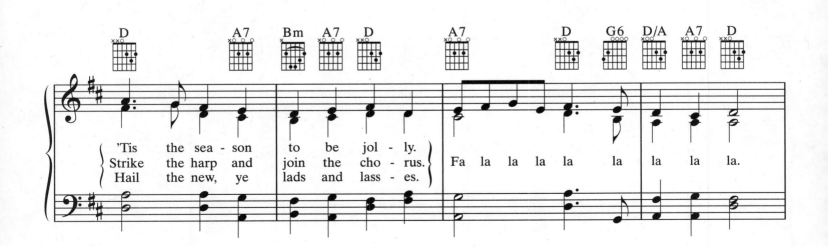

'Tis the sea - son to be jol - ly.
Strike the harp and join the cho - rus.
Hail the new, ye lads and lass - es.
Fa la la la la la la la la.

Deck the Hall - 2 - 1

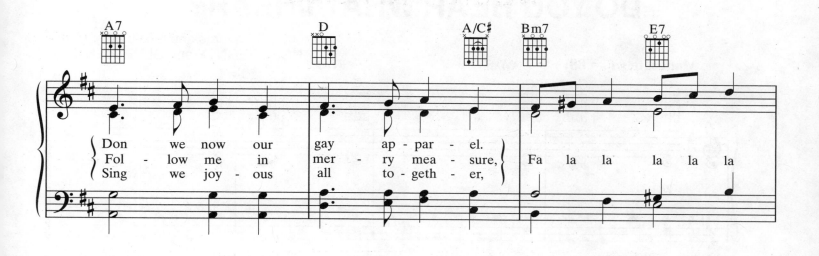

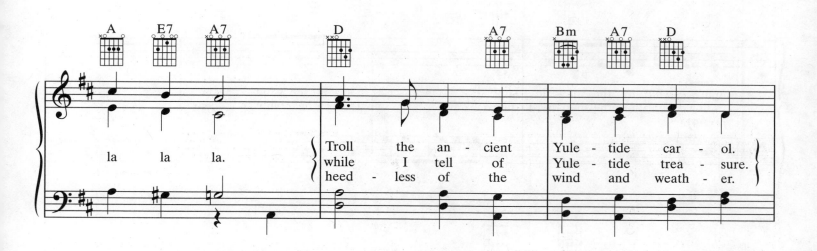

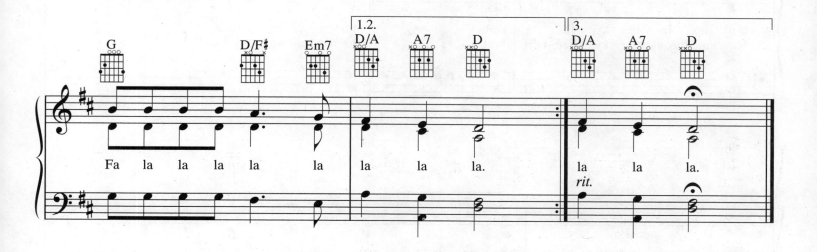

DO YOU HEAR WHAT I HEAR?

Words and Music by
NOEL REGNEY and GLORIA SHAYNE

THE FRIENDLY BEASTS

Traditional English Carol

*Optional: Use dotted bracket measures for intro.

Verse 4:
"I," said the sheep with curly horn.
"I gave Him my wool for His blanket warm.
He wore my coat on Christmas morn."
"I," said the sheep with curly horn.

Verse 5:
"I," said the dove from the rafters high.
"Cooed Him to sleep that He should not cry.
We cooed Him to sleep, my mate and I."
"I," said the dove from the rafters high.

Verse 6:
"I," said the camel, yellow and black.
"Over the desert, upon my back,
I brought Him a gift in the Wise Men's pack."
"I," said the camel, yellow and black.

Verse 7:
Thus every beast by some good spell,
In the stable dark was glad to tell
Of the gift He gave, Emmanuel,
The gift He gave, Emmanuel.

THE FIRST NOEL

Traditional English Carol

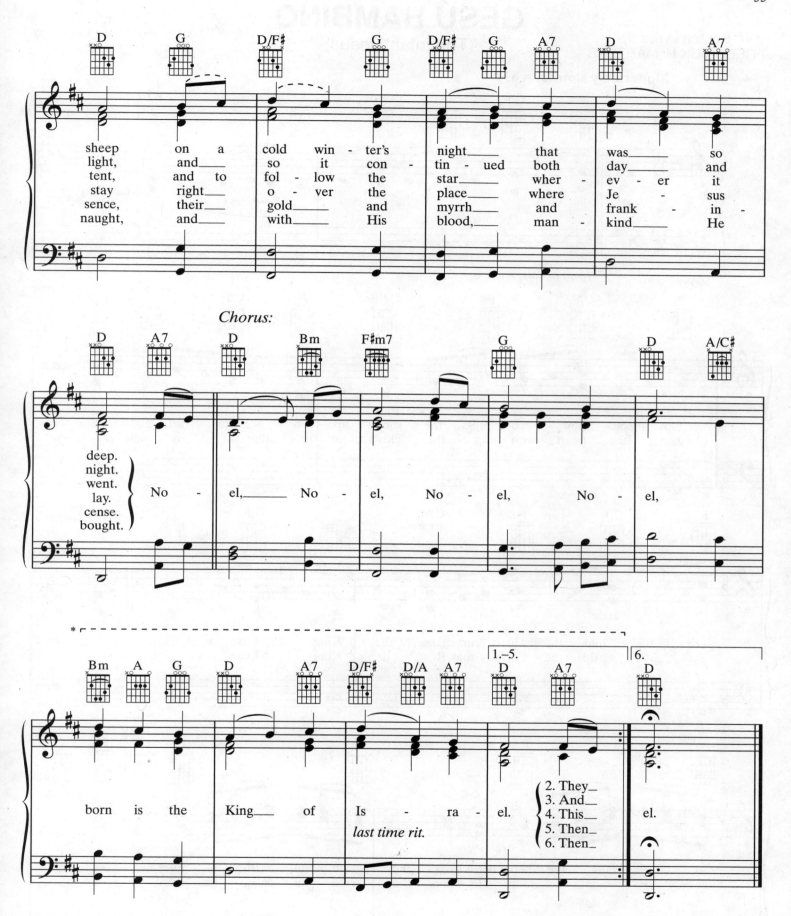

*Optional: Use dotted bracket measures for intro.

GESÚ BAMBINO
(The Infant Jesus)

English Lyrics by
FREDERICK H. MARTENS

Music and Italian Lyrics by
PIETRO A. YON

THE GIFT

Words and Music by
JIM BRICKMAN and
TOM DOUGLAS

The Gift - 4 - 1

Chorus:

GO TELL IT ON THE MOUNTAIN

Traditional Spiritual

Chorus:

Go tell it on the moun - tain, o - ver the hills, and ev - 'ry - where.

Go tell it on the moun - tain that Je - sus Christ_ is born.

{ 1. While
{ 2. The
{ 3. Down

Verse:

shep - herds kept their watch - ing o'er si - lent flocks by night, be -
shep - herds feared and trem - beled when lo! a - bove the earth rang
in a low - ly man - ger the hum - ble Christ was born. And

Go Tell It on the Mountain - 2 - 2

GOD REST YE MERRY, GENTLEMEN

Moderately, in two (♩ = 80) (♩=160)

Traditional Carol

Verse 4:
"Fear not then," said the Angel.
"Let nothing you afright.
This day is born a Savior
Of a pure Virgin bright
To free all those who trust in Him
From Satan's power and might."
(To Chorus:)

Verse 5:
The Shepherds at those tidings
Rejoiced much in mind,
And left their flocks a-feeding
In tempest, storm and wind,
And went to Bethlehem straightway,
The Son of God to find.
(To Chorus:)

Verse 6:
Now to the Lord sing praises,
All you within this place.
And with true love and brotherhood
Each other now embrace
This holy tide of Christmas.
All other doth deface.
(To Chorus:)

GOOD KING WENCESLAS

Traditional Carol

Cheerfully, in two (♩ = 74) (♩ = 148)

1. Good King Wen - ces - las looked out on the Feast of Ste - phen.
2. "Hith - er, page, and stand by me, if thou know'st it, tell - ing.
3. "Bring me flesh and bring me wine, bring me pine logs hith - er.

When the snow lay round a - bout, deep and crisp and e - ven.
Yon - der peas - ant, who is he? Where and what his dwell - ing?"
Thou and I will see him dine, when we bear him thith - er."

Bright - ly shone the moon that night, though the frost was cru - el,
"Sire, he lives a good league hence, un - der - neath the moun - tain;
Page and mon - arch forth they went, forth they went to - geth - er,

*

when a poor man came in sight, gath - 'ring win - ter fu -
Right a - gainst the for - est fence, by Saint Ag - nes' foun -
through the rude wind's wild la - ment and the bit - ter weath -

*Optional: Use dotted bracket measures for intro

*Optional: Use dotted bracket measures for intro

HARK! THE HERALD ANGELS SING

Traditional Carol

Joyfully (♩ = 104)

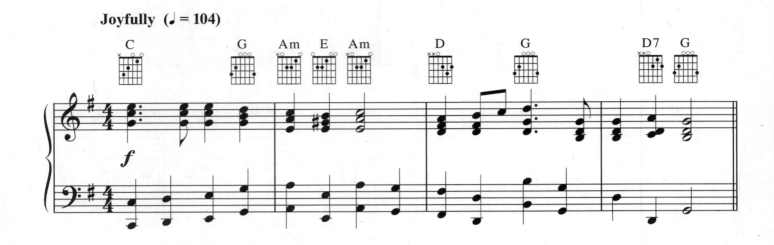

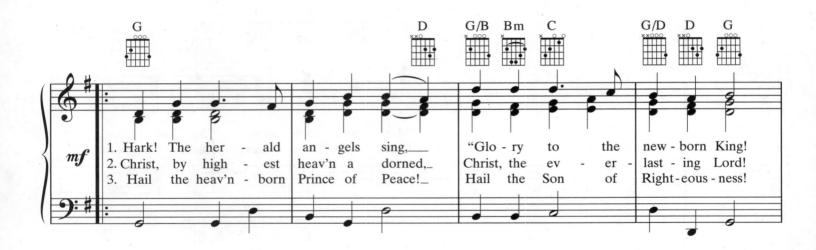

1. Hark! The her-ald an-gels sing,__ "Glo-ry to the new-born King!
2. Christ, by high-est heav'n a-dorned,__ Christ, the ev-er-last-ing Lord!
3. Hail the heav'n-born Prince of Peace!__ Hail the Son of Right-eous-ness!

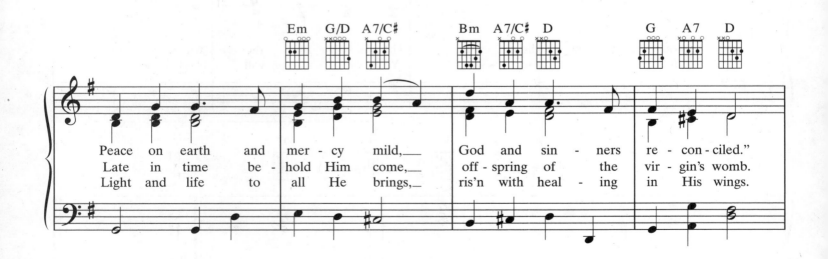

Peace on earth and mer-cy mild,__ God and sin-ners re-con-ciled."
Late in time be-hold Him come,__ off-spring of the vir-gin's womb.
Light and life to all He brings,__ ris'n with heal-ing in His wings.

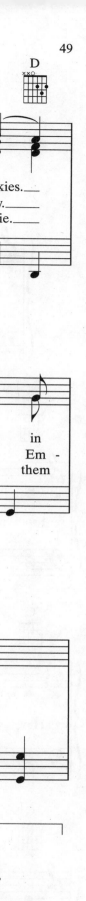

HAVE YOURSELF A
MERRY LITTLE CHRISTMAS

Words and Music by
HUGH MARTIN and RALPH BLANE

A HOLLY JOLLY CHRISTMAS

Words and Music by
JOHNNY MARKS

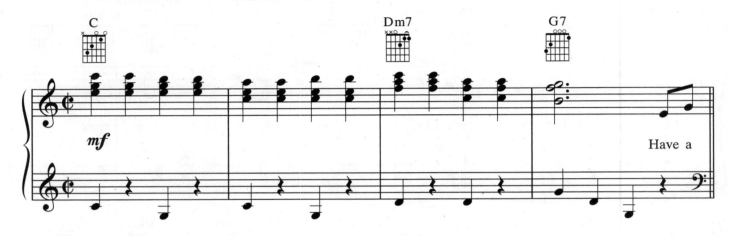

(There's No Place Like)

HOME FOR THE HOLIDAYS

Words by
AL STILLMAN

Music by
ROBERT ALLEN

Moderately, in two (♩ = 72)

Oh, there's no place like home for the hol-i-days, 'cause no mat-ter how far a-way you roam, when you pine for the sun-shine of a friend-ly gaze,

(There's No Place Like) Home for the Holidays - 3 - 1

I HEARD THE BELLS ON CHRISTMAS DAY

Words by
HENRY WADSWORTH LONGFELLOW

Music by
JOHN BAPTISTE CALKIN

I'll BE HOME FOR CHRISTMAS

Words by
KIM GANNON

Music by
WALTER KENT

62

IT CAME UPON THE MIDNIGHT CLEAR

Words by
EDMUND SEARS

Music by
RICHARD STORRS WILLIS

IT'S THE MOST WONDERFUL
TIME OF THE YEAR

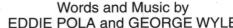

Words and Music by
EDDIE POLA and GEORGE WYLE

It's the Most Wonderful Time of the Year - 4 - 1

Bridge:

JINGLE BELLS

Words and Music by
JAMES PIERPONT

JOLLY OLD SAINT NICHOLAS

Moderately bright (♩ = 92)

Traditional American Carol

1. Jol - ly old Saint Ni - cho - las, lean your ear this way!
2. When the clock is strik - ing twelve, when I'm fast a - sleep,
3. John - ny wants a pair of skates; Su - zy wants a sled;

Don't you tell a sin - gle soul what I'm going to say.
down the chim - ney broad and black, with your pack you'll creep.
Nel - lie wants a pic - ture book, yel - low, blue and red.

Christ - mas Eve is com - ing soon. Now, you dear old man,
All the stock - ings you will find hang - ing in a row.
Now I think I'll leave to you what to give the rest.

whis - per what you'll bring to me. Tell me if you can.
Mine will be the short - est one, you'll be sure to know.
Choose for me, dear San - ta Claus, you will know the best.

*Optional: Use dotted bracket measures for intro.

JOY TO THE WORLD

Words by
ISAAC WATTS

Music by
G. F. HANDEL

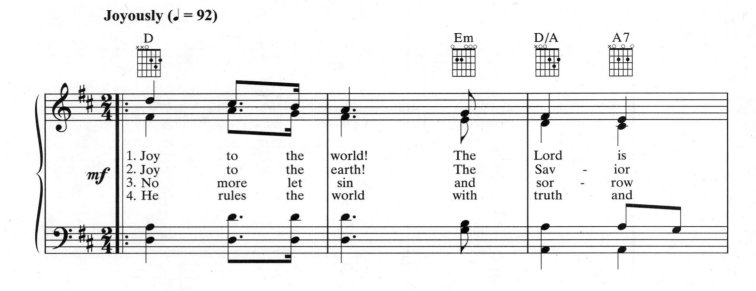

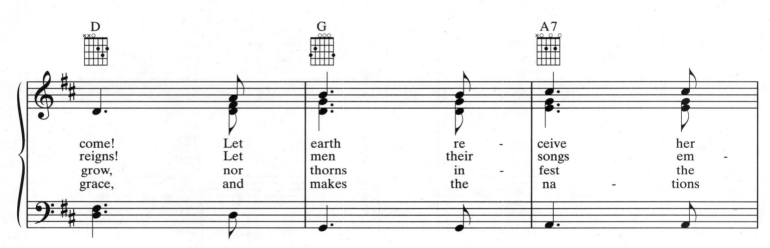

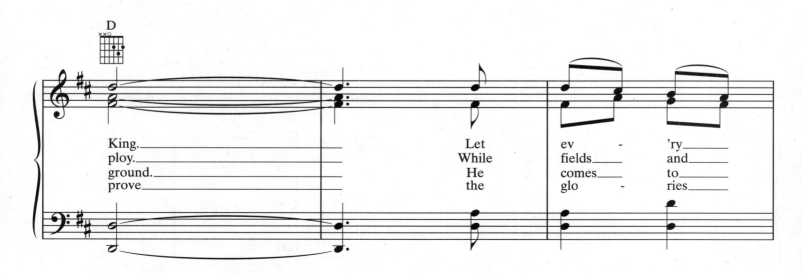

*Optional: Use dotted bracket measures for intro.

THE LITTLE DRUMMER BOY

Words and Music by
HARRY SIMEONE,
HENRY ONORATI,
and KATHERINE DAVIS

Moderately, with a march-like pulse (♩ = 56)

Verses 1 & 2:

1. Come, they told me, pa-
2. Ba - by Ge - su, pa-

rum-pum-pum - pum,_____ our new - born King to see, pa-
rum-pum-pum - pum,_____ I am a poor boy too, pa-

rum-pum-pum - pum._____ Our fi - nest gifts we bring, pa-
rum-pum-pum - pum._____ I have no gift to bring, pa-

rum-pum-pum - pum,_____ to lay be - fore the King pa-
rum-pum-pum - pum,_____ that's fit to give our King, pa-

cresc.

The Little Drummer Boy - 4 - 1

Slower (♩ = 47)

Then He smiled at me, pa - rum - pum - pum - pum,

me and my drum.

MELE KALIKIMAKA
(The Hawaiian Christmas Song)

Words and Music by
R. ALEX ANDERSON

Moderately bright (♩ = 84)

O CHRISTMAS TREE
(O Tannenbaum)

Traditional Carol

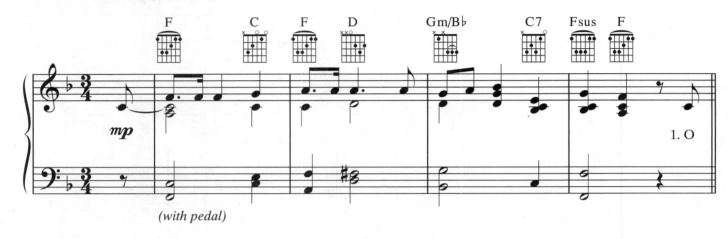

1. O

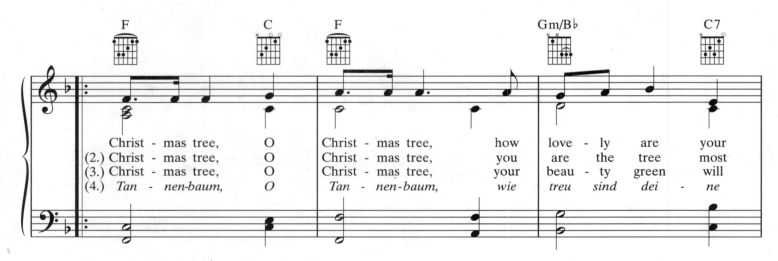

Christ - mas tree, O Christ - mas tree, how love - ly are your
(2.) Christ - mas tree, O Christ - mas tree, you are the tree your most
(3.) Christ - mas tree, O Christ - mas tree, your beau - ty green will
(4.) *Tan - nen-baum,* O *Tan - nen-baum,* *wie* *treu sind dei - ne*

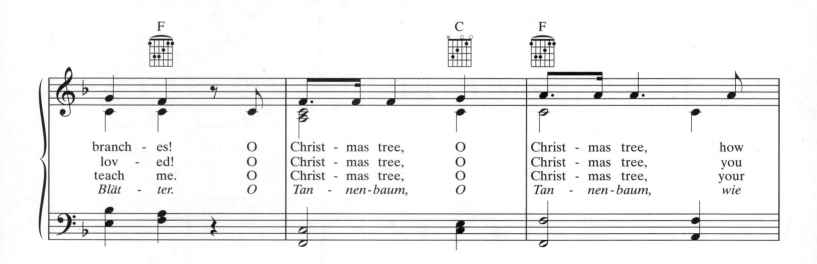

branch - es! O Christ - mas tree, O Christ - mas tree, how
lov - ed! O Christ - mas tree, O Christ - mas tree, you
teach me. O Christ - mas tree, O Christ - mas tree, your
Blät - ter. O *Tan - nen-baum,* O *Tan - nen-baum,* *wie*

O Christmas Tree (O Tannenbaum) - 2 - 1

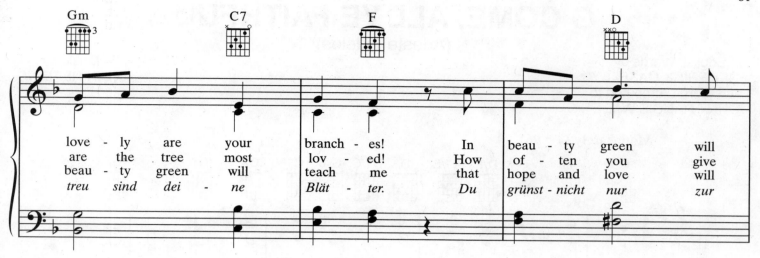

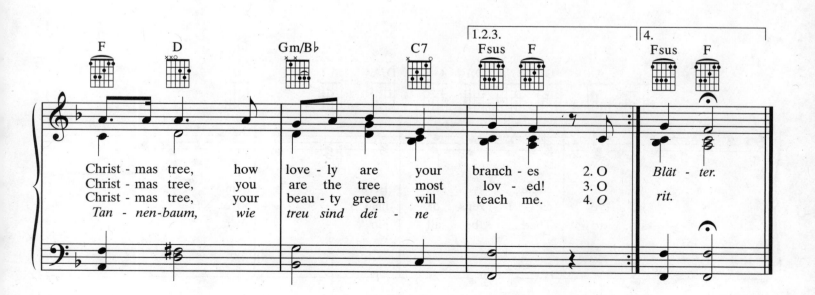

O COME, ALL YE FAITHFUL
(Adeste Fideles)

English Words by
FREDERICK OAKELEY
Latin Words Attributed to
JOHN FRANCIS WADE

Music by
JOHN READING

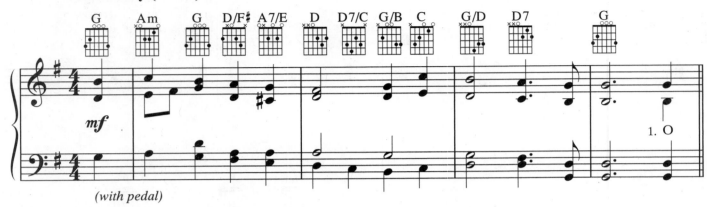

Moderately (♩ = 96)

mf

(with pedal)

1. O

Verse:

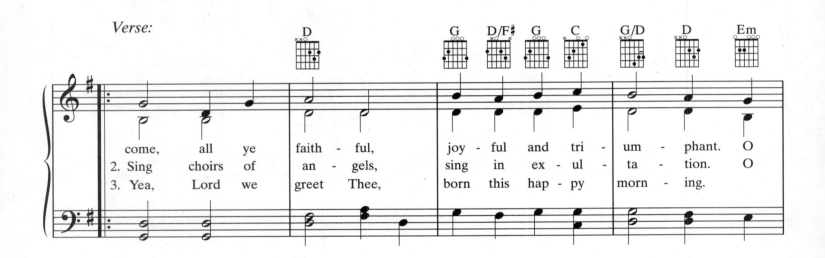

come,   all   ye   faith - ful,   joy - ful and tri - um - phant. O

2. Sing choirs of   an - gels,   sing in ex - ul - ta - tion. O

3. Yea,   Lord we   greet Thee,   born this hap - py morn - ing.

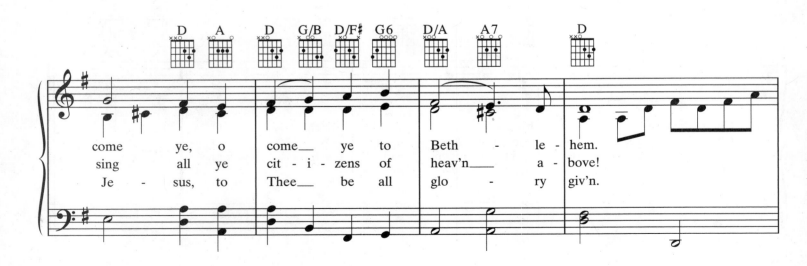

come ye, o   come ye to   Beth - le - hem.

sing all ye   cit - i - zens of   heav'n a - bove!

Je - sus, to   Thee be all   glo - ry giv'n.

Chorus:

1.2.

3.

O HOLY NIGHT

Words and Music by
J.S. DWIGHT and ADOLPHE ADAM

Slowly and solemnly ♩. = 60

1. O ho-ly night!__ The stars are bright-ly
2. .Led by the light__ of faith se-rene-ly
3. Tru-ly He taught__ us to love one an-

shin - ing, it is the night of our dear Sav-ior's birth.
beam - ing, with glow-ing heart by His cra-dle we stand.
oth - er; His law is love and His gos-pel is peace.

Long lay the world__ in sin and sor-row pin - ing, till He ap-
So led by light of a star__ sweet-ly gleam - ing, here came the
Chains shall He break, for the slave__ is our broth - er, and in His

ROCKIN' AROUND THE CHRISTMAS TREE

Words and Music by
JOHNNY MARKS

O LITTLE TOWN OF BETHLEHEM

Words by
PHILLIPS BROOKS

Music by
LEWIS H. REDNER

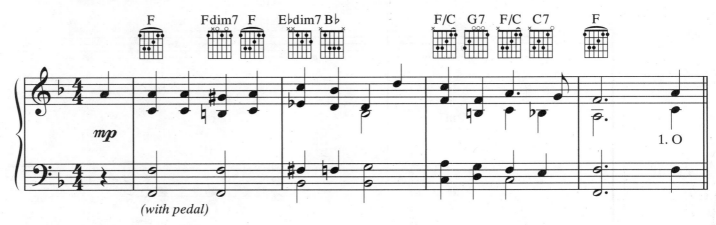

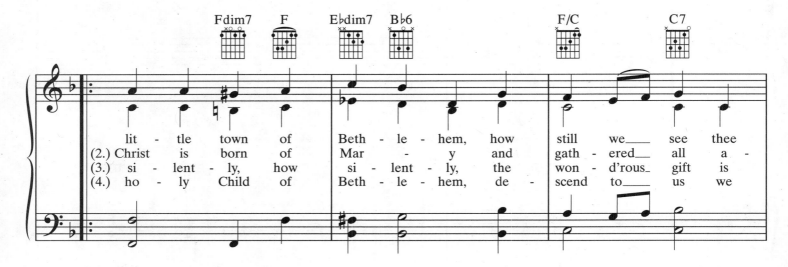

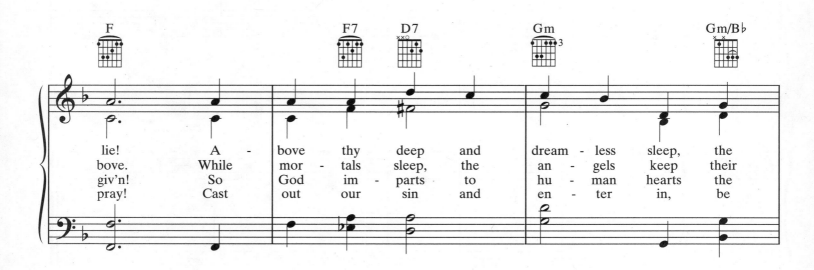

RUDOLPH, THE RED-NOSED REINDEER

Words and Music by
JOHNNY MARKS

SLEIGH RIDE

Words by
MITCHELL PARISH

Music by
LEROY ANDERSON

SANTA CLAUS IS COMIN' TO TOWN

Words by
HAVEN GILLESPIE

Music by
J. FRED COOTS

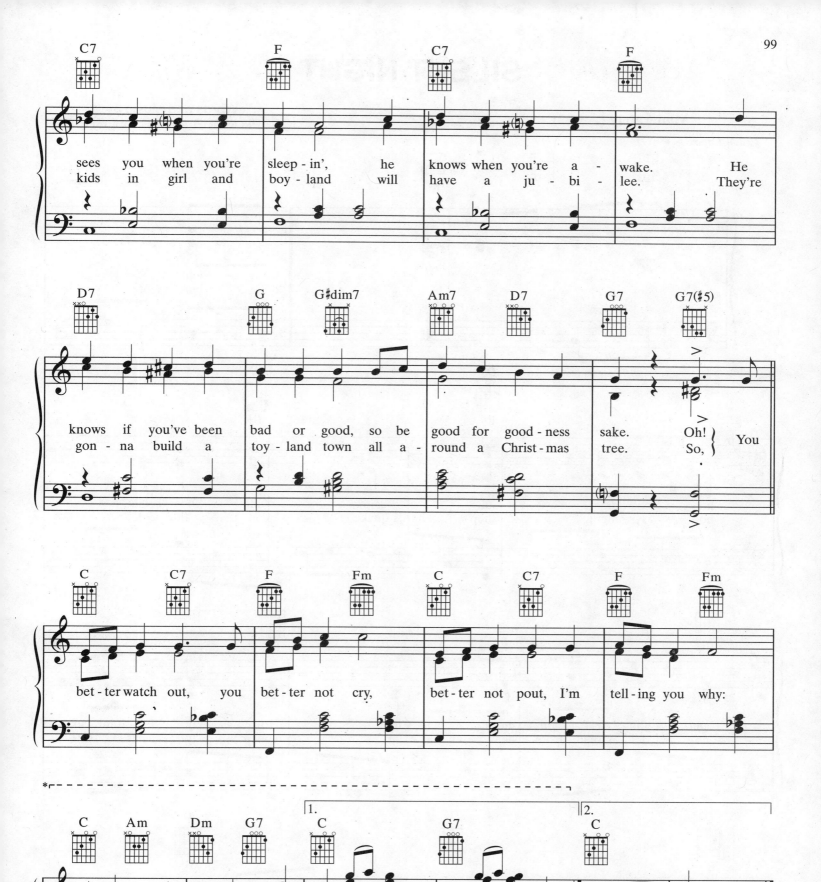

*Optional: Use dotted bracket measures for intro.

SILENT NIGHT

Words and Music by
JOSEPH MOHR and FRANZ GRUBER

1. Si - lent night,
2. Si - lent night,

ho - ly night,   all   is calm,   all   is bright,
ho - ly night,   shep - herds quake   at   the sight.

'round   yon vir - gin   moth - er and Child.   Ho - ly   In - fant, so
Glo - ries   stream from   heav - en a - far,   heav'n - ly   hosts sing,

ten - der and mild,   sleep   in heav - en - ly   peace,
"Al - le - lu - ia."   Christ,   the Sav - ior is   born.

Silent Night - 2 - 1

SILVER AND GOLD

Words and Music by
JOHNNY MARKS

TEXT ME MERRY CHRISTMAS

Words and Music by
DAVID JAVERBAUM and
ADAM SCHLESINGER

Freely (♩ = 116)

This hol-i-day you'll be far a-way,___ and I'll be all___ a-lone. So, please re-mem-ber this De-cem-ber to ful-ly charge___ your phone. And...

Moderately fast ♩ = 152

Verse:

1. Text me Mer-ry Christ-mas. Let me know you care.___
2. Text me Mer-ry Christ-mas, make my hol-i-day com-plete.___
3. Text me Mer-ry Christ-mas. Send a sel-fie, too.___

Text Me Merry Christmas - 5 - 1

THE TWELVE DAYS OF CHRISTMAS

Traditional English Carol

Moderately bright (♩ = 120)

Verse 1:
1. On the first day of Christ-mas, my true love sent to me a par - tridge_ in a pear tree.

Verse 2:
2. On the sec-ond day of Christ-mas, my true love sent to me, two tur - tle doves and a par - tridge_ in a pear tree.

Verse 3:
3. On the third day of Christ-mas, my true love sent to me, three French_hens, two tur - tle doves and a par - tridge_ in a pear tree. 4. On the

*Optional: Use dotted bracket measures for intro.

110

UKRAINIAN BELL CAROL

Composed by
MYKOLA LEONTOVYCH

Ukrainian Bell Carol - 3 - 1

WHEN CHRISTMAS COMES TO TOWN

(from *The Polar Express*)

Words by
GLEN BALLARD

Music by
ALAN SILVESTRI

When Christmas Comes to Town - 3 - 1

WE THREE KINGS OF ORIENT ARE

Words and Music by
JOHN H. HOPKINS

Moderately, not too slow (♩ = 140)

Verse:

1. We three kings of O - ri - ent are,
2. Born a king of Beth - le - hem's plain,
3. Frank - in - cense to of - fer have I,
4. Myrrh is mine, its bit - ter per - fume
5. Glo - rious now be - hold Him a - rise,

bear - ing gifts we trav - erse a - far;
gold I bring to crown Him a - gain;
in - cense owns a De - i - ty nigh.
breathes of life of gath - er - ing gloom;
King and God and sac - ri - fice.

field and foun - tain, moor and moun - tain
King for ev - er, ceas - ing nev - er,
Pray'r and prais - ing, all men rais - ing,
sor - r'ring, sigh - ing, bleed - ing, dy - ing,
Al - le - lu - ia, al - le - lu - ia,

WE WISH YOU A MERRY CHRISTMAS

Traditional English Folk Song

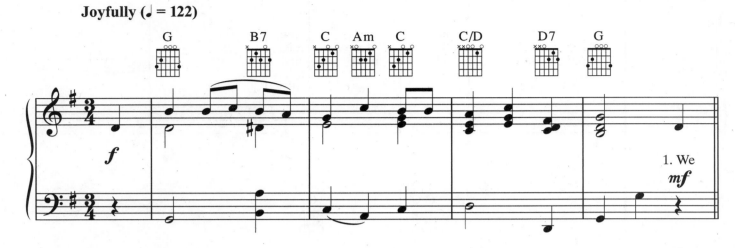

Verses 1– 4:

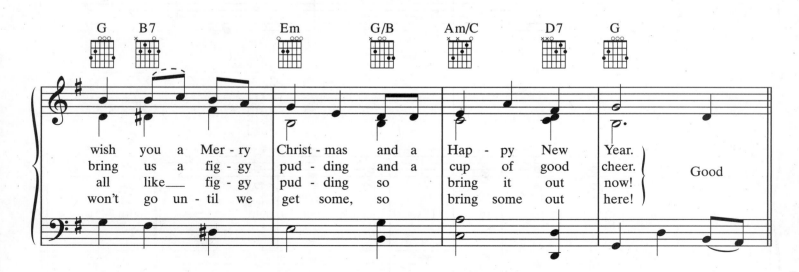

WELCOME CHRISTMAS

(from *How the Grinch Stole Christmas*)

Lyrics by
DR. SEUSS

Music by
ALBERT HAGUE

WHAT CHILD IS THIS?
(Greensleeves)

By WILLIAM C. DIX
Old English Air

Gently (♪ = 104)

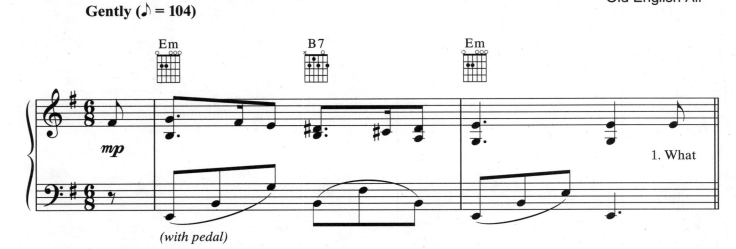

(with pedal)

1. What

Verse:

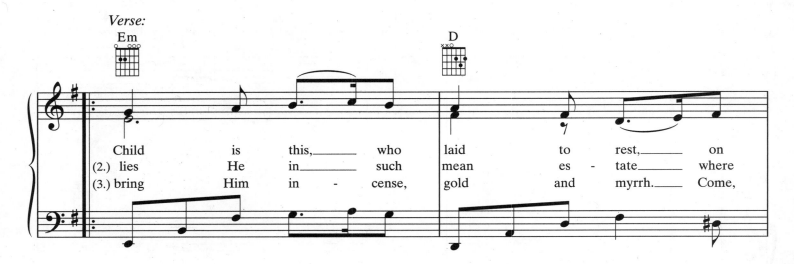

Child is this,___ who laid to rest,___ on
(2.) lies He in___ such mean es - tate___ where
(3.) bring Him in - cense, gold and myrrh.___ Come,

Mar - y's lap___ is sleep - ing? Whom an - gels greet___ with
ox and ass___ are feed - ing? Good Chris - tian, fear,___ for
peas - ant king,___ to own___ Him. The King of Kings___ sal -

YOU'RE A MEAN ONE, MR. GRINCH
(from *How the Grinch Stole Christmas*)

Lyrics by
DR. SEUSS

Music by
ALBERT HAGUE

Moderate swing (♩ = 104)

Verses 1 & 2:

mean one,   Mis-ter   Grinch,   you   real - ly   are   a   heel.   You're as   Your
mon - ster,   Mis-ter   Grinch.   You're   heart's an   emp - ty   hole.

cud - dly   as   a   cac - tus   and   as   charm - ing   as   an   eel,   Mis - ter   Grinch.
brain   is   full   of   spi - ders,   you   got   gar - lic   in   your   soul,   Mis - ter   Grinch.

1.

You're a   bad   ba - na - na   with a   greas-y   black   peel.
I   would-n't   touch   you   with   a

You're a Mean One, Mr. Grinch - 2 - 1